I Love
GOD
Because...

Illustrations by Herald Entertainment, Inc.
Printed in China
First Printing: June 2018
ISBN: 978-1-947774-74-2

I love God because He created me.

I love God because
He created an amazing world.

I love God because He made pets!

I love God because
He made really fun things
— like laughter.

I love God because
He made friends
and family!

I love God because He made yummy things that can be used to make even more yummy things!

I love God because
He watches
over me,
day...

...and night.

I love God because He's never too busy to listen to me.

I love God because He gave me imagination!

I love God because
He knows how silly I can be and
He loves me anyway!

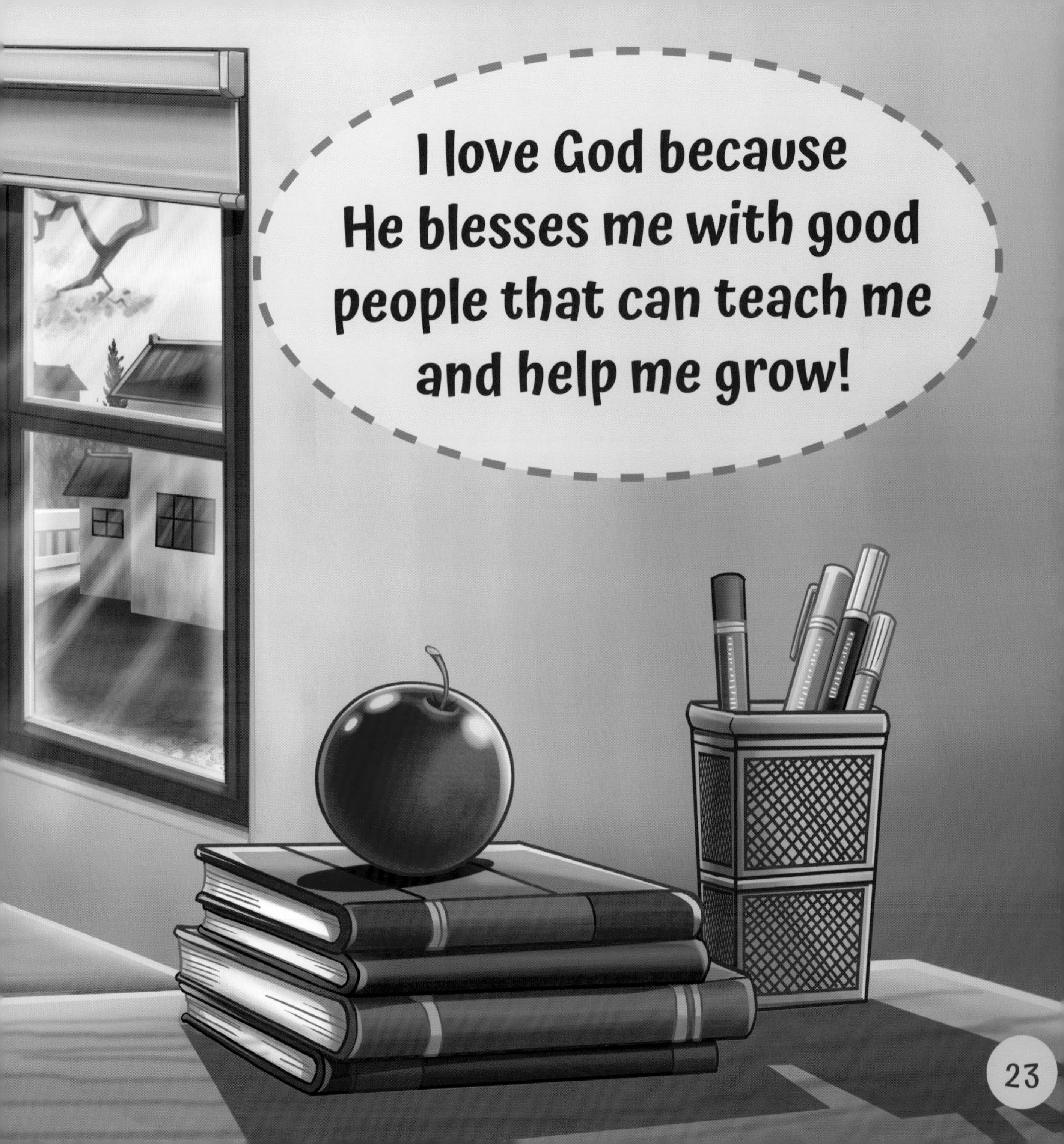
I love God because
He blesses me with good
people that can teach me
and help me grow!

I love God because
He sent His Son, Jesus!

I love God because His Son, Jesus, died for me and then rose again!

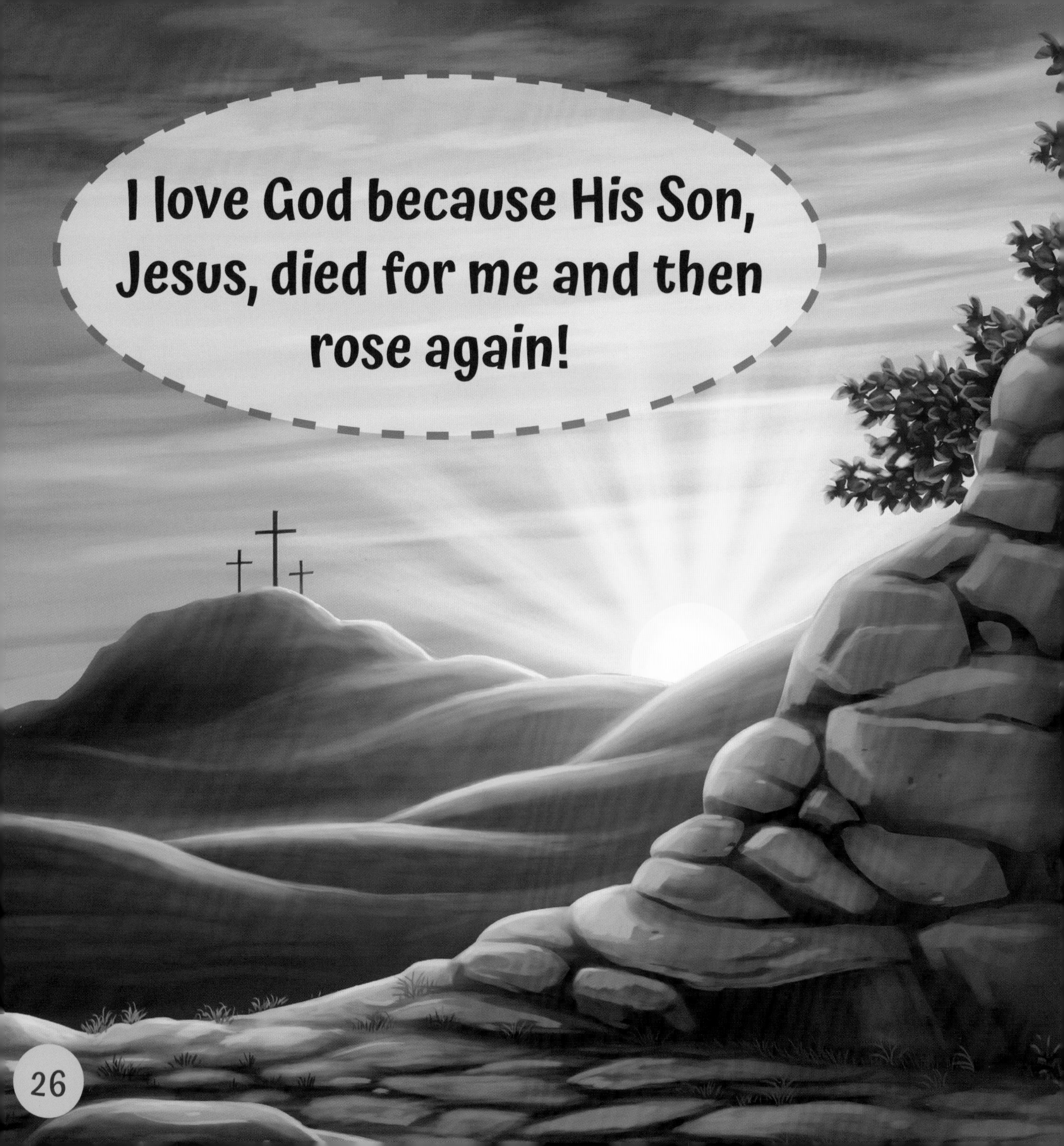

I love God because
He made heaven, where
I can be with Him forever!

I Love God.

"It is good
to praise the Lord."

Psalm 92:1

in English & Spanish !
The JESUS STORIES
Vol. 1
3
Episodes!

in English & Spanish !
The JESUS STORIES
Vol. 2
3
Episodes!